All About Your Gerbil

Contents

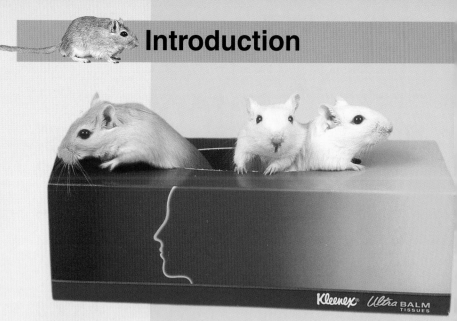

Gerbils are hardy. inexpensive to keep, and entertaining to watch at work and at play.

DID YOU KNOW?

Mongolian gerbils were first recorded in the wild on the 14th of April 1866 by the French biologist Abb David, who was travelling through Mongolia and China. He wrote the following entry in his diary... "This morning I acquired three yellow rats I do not yet know the name of, having long hairy tails."

If you own gerbils, or are thinking of getting some, this book is for you. It aims to give you the basic information you need to ensure that your little companions enjoy a healthy and happy life. As with any pet, before you take it on, it is important to think about the time, effort and expense that is needed to look after your pet for the whole of its life. Although gerbils are often looked after by children, they must receive proper care and attention even when the novelty of a new arrival has worn off. Fortunately, the gerbil is a pretty low-maintenance pet that does not make too many demands on its owner.

The Perfect Pet

Gerbils (or more accurately, the Mongolian gerbil) are ideal for someone wanting a small mammal as a pet for many reasons:

- They are hardy, and inexpensive to keep.
- They are normally active during the day, unlike hamsters, who wake up just as their owners are going to sleep.
- They are sociable little creatures that appreciate being kept in groups, provided that they grow up together.
- They are very entertaining to watch at work and at play, but can also become very tame if they are handled regularly from a young age.
- They are not generally aggressive with people, and only bite under extreme duress.
- They are very clean, and do not smell if properly kept.

Understanding Gerbils

In the wild, the Mongolian gerbil lives in harsh semi-desert conditions, with great temperature variations between summer and winter, and night and day. Gerbils protect themselves from this by burrowing underground, building a complex system of storage chambers, which are used to store food through the long winters when the ground may be covered in deep snow.

Gerbils feed on grasses, crops of wheat and millet and sometimes insects. They conserve body fluids by not sweating, and producing very small amounts of concentrated urine and dry faeces.

The gerbil is one of the cleanest pets to keep.

Breeds

Golden Agouti

The standard colouring of a gerbil is golden agouti, with a sandy body colour, paler hair underneath and a line of darker hairs down the back and along the tail, which also has a black tip.

The golden agouti has a sandy body colour, and darker hairs along the back and the tail.

Colour Varieties

There are a few colour varieties that have been selectively bred:

Albino

There is body pigment at all, and they are completely white with pink eyes.

Black

There are abnormal amounts of dark pigment in the body.

The black gerbil has abnormal amounts of dark pigment in the body.

Dove

A lighter grey in colour.

White Spot

A similar body colour to the golden agouti, but, as the name suggests, it has white patches on the head and body.

Cinnamon

This is similar to the golden agouti, but lacks the darker hairs on its body.

These colour variations have been selected from mutations that have occurred as gerbils have been bred since they were first domesticated about thirty years ago, and, no doubt, more will follow. The choice of coat colour is entirely a matter of personal preference, as there is no difference in terms of their suitability as pets.

DID YOU KNOW?

The normal life expectancy for a gerbil is just two or three years, but the oldest recorded pet gerbil was Sahara, who belonged to Aaron Milstone of Michigan, USA and died at the age of eight years four months in October 1981.

Set up the accommodation before you purchase your gerbils, so they will be able to settle quickly into their new home. When it comes to keeping gerbils, wire cages are *out*, and glass gerbilariums are definitely *in*. So what is a gerbilarium, and why is it the best way to keep them?

Gerbilarium

A gerbilarium is an all-glass aquarium with a close-fitting, wire-mesh top, but instead of being filled with water, it is filled to about half its depth with alternate layers of peat and chopped straw or wood chippings. The tank should be at least 75cms (30ins) long, 40cms (16ins) wide, and 30cms (12ins) deep, but a larger one is necessary if you want to keep more than one pair of gerbils.

Peat and chopped straw can be layered inside the gerbilarium.

With this set-up, you can create surroundings that mimic the gerbil's natural environment in the wild, and you have the immense satisfaction of watching them build tunnels and nesting chambers underground. There are few opportunities to keep domestic pets in such a natural setting, and many hours can be wiled away, watching them build and maintain their home.

Do not use sand, as it is quite abrasive and can cause sores to develop on the face.

Bedding

You need to provide some bedding material, that the gerbils will drag underground and shred up to line their nest. Whatever you use should be non-toxic and digestible, so that it will not harm the gerbils if swallowed. Clean, white tissue paper is ideal for this purpose, but there is no need to buy it ready-shredded, as the gerbils will enjoy doing the job.

Feeding Bowls

Strong ceramic bowls are best for food, as they are easily cleaned and heavy enough not to turn over too easily.

Gerbils can be kept in a gerbilarium – a glass tank with a close-fitting wire-mesh top.

Setting Up Home

A specially designed unit, with inter-connecting tunnels also makes a good home.

Water Bottle

A gravity-fed water bottle is ideal as it will reduce excessive wetting of the litter with spilt water. The bottle can be suspended over the side of the tank. Although gerbils do not drink a great deal, they should have access to a clean water supply at all times.

Jam Jar

Gerbils like to have a separate toilet area set aside for their use, and if you bury a jam jar on its side in the litter, they generally learn to use it for this purpose very quickly. This makes cleaning out very easy, as the jam jar can be lifted out the tank, washed in warm soapy water, and replaced for further use.

Handling

Gerbils are not naturally aggressive, and quickly become used to humans if they are handled regularly and gently from an early age. Approach them from the front so that they are not startled, and, at first, always pick them up over a table or a cushion so that they do not hurt themselves if they jump out of your hand.

Pick the gerbil up in cupped hands, or allow the gerbil to walk on to your hand and gently restrain it with your other hand over its back. Gerbils should not be lifted off the ground by the tail, but they can be restrained by holding the base of the tail between the fingers. If the tail is held too near the end, the skin can be stripped off.

In order to get a greater degree of restraint to carry out some procedure, you can grasp the scruff of the neck between two fingers and press gently downwards. Gerbils generally resent being held on their backs.

The correct way to hold a gerbil.

When you buy a gerbil, look for one that is clean and well-cared-for.

You can buy a gerbil from any good pet store, where experienced staff will be on hand to help you. Alternatively you may know someone locally who breeds gerbils, and you might be able to find an address of a gerbil club from your library or pet shop. You may also be able to obtain a gerbil from a friend that has breed some.

Fit And Healthy

In all instances, look for a gerbil that is clean
and well-cared-for. In a pet shop, it is a good
sign if the staff are knowledgeable and can
give advice when you are making
your choice. Resist the temptation to
buy a sickly gerbil from a pet shop
just because you feel sorry for it – you
could end up with a lot of heartache,
trouble and expense trying to get it well.

What Age?

The ideal age for purchase is six
to eight weeks. Avoid buying
gerbils at over ten weeks, as
taming may be more difficult, and
they may fight if introduced to other
gerbils.

How Many?

Buy at least a pair of gerbils, ideally two
females from the same litter, or a male and a
female from different litters if you want to
breed from them. If you have sufficiently
large accommodation, you can allow several
family pairs to live together. Eventually you
will have to separate them into single sex
groups unless you have a ready supply of
good homes for the young.

DID YOU KNOW?

Over eighty species
of gerbil exist in the
wild, differing widely
in size, colour and
length of tail. One
species, Wagner's
gerbil, feeds almost
entirely on snails.

Buying A Gerbil

Male Or Female?

Sexing gerbils when they are young can be very tricky, but is easier if you compare one with another. Hold the gerbils side by side, by the base of their tails, and gently lift their rumps off the ground. Each has an anal opening and a uro-genital one, but the space between the two is significantly greater in the male than in the female.

Gerbils become sexually mature at around three months of age, so if you do not want your gerbil to breed, the sexes should be separated at this age.

A male gerbil.

A female gerbil.

12

The Signs Of a Healthy Gerbil

A healthy gerbil should normally be bright and active. Look for the following signs when you select a new gerbil.

- _Eyes:_ bright and clear, without any discharge

- _Mouth:_ clean. Dribbling can be a sign of problems

- _Nose:_ clean and free of discharge

- _Coat:_ well-groomed. Should not be soiled or matted

- _Breathing:_ quiet and regular. Should not be laboured

- _Body condition:_ well-covered and rounded. No abnormal swellings.

Gerbils
should be fed a mixture of seeds, such as sunflower, wheat, millet, maize, oats and barley. Balanced seed mixtures, specifically for gerbils can be purchased, and each gerbil should be fed about one tablespoonful daily. They do not hoard food when kept in captivity – it seems this behaviour is only triggered in the wild when the temperature falls. So feed one meal each day, and remove uneaten food at the end of that day.

Make sure that your gerbils do not get 'hooked' on a single food such as sunflower seeds, as this can be harmful. If this happens, impose a strict limit on the quantities of any one food. Complete pelleted foods, such as those available for feeding laboratory rats and mice, are also fine for gerbils.

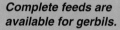

Complete feeds are available for gerbils.

A Menu For Gerbils

Complete foods may supply the basic needs of pet gerbils, but a variety of food provides interest for both the animal and its owner, since we all get enjoyment from seeing the pleasure that a special treat may give. Here are some of the things your gerbils may choose for their picnic hamper – but don't let them over-indulge ....

- Apple and other fruit is appreciated occasionally.
  - Green vegetables such as sprouts, cabbage and hay.
- Clover, Dandelion and groundsel – well-washed, fresh from the garden.
  - Grated cheese – in small quantities.
  - Raisins, melon seeds and unsalted peanuts.
- Hard-boiled egg – just a little from time to time.

Dandelion leaves

If you are giving your gerbil a varied diet, or a complete food that has been well made up, there should be no need to add extra vitamins and minerals. If you are concerned that your pet may not be getting enough of these, especially at times when they need extra, such as when they are growing, or rearing their young, a tiny pinch of a balanced small animal supplement, from a vet or pet shop, can be sprinkled on food a couple of times a week.

Treats

Some edible treats also provide entertainment for your gerbils. They will enjoy wrestling with a large, thin slice of apple or carrot. Twigs from fruit trees are safe for gerbils to gnaw, so long as they have not recently been sprayed with pesticide. Avoid softwoods such as pine, and branches from trees that could be poisonous such as laburnum and holly.

Groundsel

Gerbils are highly active, and are able to jump, climb and burrow with great expertise. In the wild they may travel long distances in their search for food, so in captivity they need the space and the facilities to exercise regularly. In a well-set-up gerbilarium they will achieve this by digging their underground warrens and scurrying around.

Exercise Wheels

If your gerbils are living in a cage, you will need to provide an exercise wheel. Those designed for golden hamsters are not always suitable, due to the smaller size of the gerbil and the tendency for their tail to get caught.

Your gerbil will enjoy exploring his home, crawling through the tunnels. If you provide an exercise wheel, make sure it is the solid, plastic type without spokes.

Use a solid, plastic wheel without spokes, of a suitable size. Some gerbils seem to get quite addicted to using them, in which case you should only allow them to work out for limited periods.

Running Free

Letting gerbils out to exercise indoors is an option, but they are excellent escape artists. Many a gerbil has set up home inside an old settee, entering through a hole in the upholstery! Ensure all other animals are excluded from the room, and all hiding places and escape routes are blocked off. Tempt your gerbils back home with a tasty titbit if all else fails.

Toys

A wide range of toys are available, but the best toys are often the simplest and cheapest. A terracotta flower pot makes a good gerbil hideaway. First, make a hole in the rim for the gerbil to get in and out, and then stand it upside down. Make sure there are no sharp edges that could cause injury. Plastic flower pots should be avoided as they may splinter when gnawed.

Wooden gnaws will help to keep your gerbil's teeth in trim.

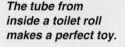

An all-time favourite is the cardboard tube from inside a toilet roll – a sort of 'eat your own tunnel', which the gerbils will enjoy destroying once they have finished running in and out of it. A cardboard egg box or a wooden cotton-reel can also provide hours of fun. A block of wood, with all the splinters sanded off, or a piece of fruit tree branch, will serve as a good gnawing block and will help to keep the teeth in trim. The gerbils will also enjoy clambering over the branch.

Don't put in too many new playthings at any one time – the gerbils will appreciate it much more if they only have two or three items in the cage at any one time, and they are changed every few days.

The tube from inside a toilet roll makes a perfect toy.

A hidey-hole log will provide lots of entertainment.

There are no vaccinations that you can give your gerbil to prevent diseases, in the way that you can with pet cats and dogs. Fortunately, gerbils are pretty sturdy, low-maintenance pets, and as long as they are provided with suitable food and housing, as described in this book, problems are rare.

Cleaning the Gerbilarium

Because gerbils produce such small quantities of urine and very dry faeces, a gerbilarium does not need cleaning out very often, particularly if they are trained to use a 'toilet jar', as described earlier. Indeed, the gerbils will be annoyed at having their carefully constructed habitation destroyed.

Therefore, the bedding should only be changed every three or four months, unless it becomes particularly soiled before then. You can take the opportunity to wash out the tank at this stage.

The water bottle must be refilled every day.

Caring For Your Gerbil

Tips For Tidiness

The gerbillarium can be kept as clean as possible in the interim by:-

● Not feeding excessive amounts of perishable foods.
● Removing any uneaten fruit and vegetables at the end of each day.
● Empty and refill the water bottle each day, making sure it is not leaking on to the litter.

Teeth

Gerbil's teeth grow all the time, but they wear down naturally providing that they have plenty of things to gnaw on. If the diet does not provide sufficient dental exercise, the teeth may become overgrown. If this happens, the gerbil will show signs of discomfort around his mouth, and the teeth may need to be cut back by a vet.

Gerbils teeth grow all the time, so they must be provided with gnawing material.

Nails

Gerbils generally keep their toenails short by digging and scrabbling around their cage, but they may occasionally become overgrown. Because gerbils are so small and wriggly, clipping the nails is not an easy job, and should be carried out by an expert

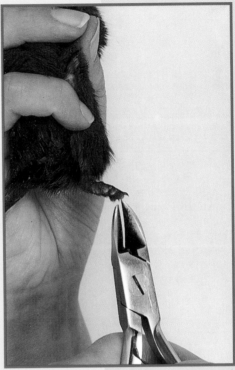

If your gerbil's nails become overgrown, you should seek the help of an expert who can trim them for you.

21

Breeding

When reared in pairs in a suitable environment, the main problem with gerbils is not getting them to breed, but persuading them to stop. One pair can easily produce thirty or forty young in a year, and since they sexually mature at around three months of age, you don't have to be a brilliant mathematician to work out that this can equal an awful lot of gerbils within the reproductive lifetime of one female, which is about twenty months. The only practicable way to prevent them from breeding is to separate them into single sex pairs.

Mating

Mating is noisy and boisterous, with the male stamping his hind feet on the ground and chasing after the female, alternately mounting her and then grooming himself. Pregnancy lasts about 24 days, during which time the female should only be handled very gently. Gerbils will make their own nests underground, so as long as you provide some plain, white, tissue paper to be torn up as bedding, there is no need to provide a nesting box if they are kept in a gerbilarium rather than a cage.

DID YOU KNOW?

Although we think of rodents as being small, the largest is the South American capybara, or water hog, that has a body length of about four feet and can weigh up to 113kg, or 250 pounds.

DID YOU KNOW?

Over fifty per cent of all the species of mammals are rodents, named after the Latin word rodere, meaning 'to gnaw'. This is because all rodents have one pair of upper and one pair of lower incisor teeth at the front of their mouth that grow continually and wear against each other as they gnaw at their food.

The Young

The young are born very under-developed - blind, hairless and with a dark-red skin colour. There are usually around six in a litter, and the parents should be allowed to look after them relatively undisturbed for the first three or four weeks. The babies develop very quickly, and by the end of the first week they are beginning to explore. Hair starts to grow at six days of age, the eyes open at ten to twelve days, and by four weeks of age they are fully independent.

Breeding

Development

The young can be housed together until six to eight weeks of age, at which time they will need to be rehomed. About a quarter of the young that are weaker than the others may well die before weaning, and although this may be distressing, it is a natural process that has to be accepted as normal.

Special Needs

Pregnant gerbils, and those nursing their young, will need a greater quantity of food each day, and also extra protein, given in the form of cheese, hard-boiled eggs, and even a little dog or cat food. Give a balanced gerbil vitamin and mineral supplement sprinkled on the food.

The youngsters can be weaned at three to four weeks of age on to fine food such as canary seeds and a little washed fruit and vegetables.

It is possible for the female to become pregnant almost immediately after giving birth, and since she will suckle the young for up to four weeks, she may have her next litter immediately after weaning the last. In this case, the young should be separated from her when they are about 22 days old to allow her at least a couple of days rest.

Provide white tissue paper which can be used as bedding.

Gerbils will normally store their food away underground, so it is possible to leave a gerbil unattended for two or three days, provided there is a good supply of food and water. Only a small amount of perishable food such as fruit and green vegetable should be left.

If your gerbils are left for a longer period, you may be able to board them with a vet, a pet shop, or perhaps a breeder.

Make sure that whoever looks after your gerbils knows all about their requirements, and leave the contact number of your veterinary surgeon in case a problem should arise.

A gerbil can be left on its own for a couple of days, provided there is a good supply of food and water.

First Aid

If your gerbil is seriously unwell, your veterinary surgeon must be contacted without delay for assistance. Although children often care for gerbils, it is necessary for a responsible adult to take the gerbil along and authorise any treatment needed.

Most small animal veterinary practices see a large number of small mammals and are very willing and able to treat them. It is even possible to anaesthetise gerbils to carry out surgical operations such as tumour removal or amputation of a badly damaged limb, although the risks are greater than for a cat or a dog undergoing a similar procedure.

Administering Medication

The most important care for a sick or injured gerbil is to keep it warm and administer fluids to try and prevent dehydration, which can

DID YOU KNOW?

Gerbils are sometimes referred to as jirds.

occur quite quickly. A dropper or a small syringe is ideal for administering solutions, but do not use excessive force. Remember, that fluids can cause more harm than good if they are inhaled.

Commercial rehydration powders that are designed to be made up with water can be purchased from a vet or a chemist, but a gerbil will only take a few drops at a time. Alternatively, you can use boiled tap-water that has been allowed to cool, with a heaped tablespoonful of glucose powder and a level teaspoonful of salt per pint (450 mls) added.

Injuries

Small wounds can be gently flushed with warm water and treated with a mild antiseptic, but any major injuries will require veterinary attention. It is very common for an over-active gerbil to fall off a high surface.

If this happens, gently return the gerbil to its nest to recover from the shock. If it is not improving within an hour, it may have broken some bones or suffered internal injuries, and will need to see a vet.

Visiting a Vet

A gerbil can be cupped gently in two hands to pick it up, and then transferred to a small cardboard or perspex box, with plenty of bedding to keep it warm during its journey. It is most unlikely that a poorly gerbil would eat through a cardboard box during the journey, but it should be supervised at all times, just in case.

Treating gerbils

Gerbils are not the easiest of patients, partly because of their small size, and partly because of the way they react to certain drugs. There are almost no products that have been developed and tested for use in gerbils, because the market is simply not big enough to make it financially viable for a drug company. Therefore, a vet has to use products that are available for use in other species of animal, or even human medicines. This makes the use of any drug more unpredictable in gerbils than in many other animals. Dosing a gerbil with medicine is quite difficult, although it can sometimes be managed with drops of a liquid medicine. A gerbil may refuse to drink water that has been treated, particularly when it is unwell. A course of injections is often the safest way to ensure a gerbil does receive a proper course of treatment, but this does involve repeated visits to the vet.

Signs of ill health

Your gerbil is probably unwell if it exhibiting any of the following signs:

- Not eating
- Lethargy
- Laboured breathing
- Sores anywhere on the body
- Loose droppings
- Abnormal lumps and bumps

Common Ailments

Abscesses

These may develop on the body as a result of injuries on sharp objects, from fighting with other gerbils, or within the mouth as a result of tooth problems. They consist of raw, smelly, discharging areas that have become infected by bacteria, and will usually need antibiotic treatment from a vet. If the gerbil will tolerate it, regular bathing of the affected areas with a solution of one teaspoonful of salt in a pint of warm water will help to keep them clean.

Cancers

These are very common in older gerbils, occurring in many possible sites around the body, but can only rarely be treated by surgical removal.

Diarrhoea

This is less common in gerbils than in many other small mammals such as hamsters. However, gerbils kept in colonies can be affected by Tyzzers disease and Salmonellosis, both caused by bacteria and both potentially transmissible to humans. Tyzzers disease can sometimes be so severe that the gerbils are simply found dead without any obvious cause externally.

Mild cases of diarrhoea will usually respond to a change to a bland diet, but strict hygienic precautions should be observed when handling affected animals, and veterinary attention sought if the problem is severe or does not respond to more conservative management.

Epilepsy ●─────

Some gerbils will go into a short convulsion when subjected to sudden stress, such as loud noises or unaccustomed handling. There is no treatment needed, other than trying to avoid the triggering factors, but it seems to be hereditary, so affected animals should not be used for breeding.

Eye and nose problems ●

Gerbils sometimes suffer from sore eyes and nose caused by excessive gnawing and burrowing, especially if they are gnawing at the wire-mesh of a cage, or if the litter is dirty or unsuitable. A veterinary surgeon will be able to prescribe an antibiotic and anti-inflammatory ointment to treat the problem, but it is essential to identify the cause and correct it.

Heat exhaustion ●─────

Gerbils use behavioural changes to keep themselves cool, such as burrowing deeper underground. If the temperature rises and they are unable to take the necessary action, they can easily suffer from heat exhaustion, especially if their glass gerbilarium is left in direct sunlight. They will lie still in their cage, trembling slightly. If this happens, the gerbils should be moved immediately to a darkened and well-ventilated room to recover. Make sure they have a plentiful supply of fresh water.

Poisoning

Gerbils are quite sensitive to poisoning, particularly because they spend a lot of time grooming and will lick off any substances that get on to their coat. Take great care not to use aerosol sprays in the room where the gerbil lives, unless you have checked that they are non-toxic to animals.

Skin problems

Infectious skin problems are not common in gerbils kept as pets, because they generally have very little opportunity to come into contact with other gerbils. It is possible for them to suffer from ringworm, a fungus that grows on the hairs, and can also cause skin problems in humans and other animals.

Gerbils have glands on the underside of their belly that secrete a scent used as a territory marker. These can sometimes become infected, inflamed and sore, in which case a vet may need to prescribe an anti-inflammatory and antibiotic ointment.